The Library of Living and Working in Colonial Times™

A Day in the Life of a Colonial Indigo Planter

Laurie Krebs

The Rosen Publishing Group's
PowerKids Press™
New York

For my friend, Claire Carlson
With thanks to Nicole Green, South Carolina Room, Charleston County Public Library

Published in 2004 by The Rosen Publishing Group, Inc.
29 East 21st Street, New York, NY 10010

First Edition

Editor: Frances E. Ruffin
Book Design: Emily Muschinske
Layout Design: Eric DePalo

Photo Credits: Cover, title page (indigo), p. 8 (background) © Kirsten Soderlind/CORBIS; cover, title page and p. 11(inset) courtesy of the Irma and Paul Milstein Division of United States History, Local History and Genealogy, The New York Public Library, Astor, Lenox, and Tilden Foundations; p. 4 Collection of the Museum of Early Southern Decorative Arts; p. 7 (foreground) courtesy of the National Museum of American History, Smithsonian Institution; p. 7 (background) courtesy of the Fenimore Art Museum, Cooperstown, New York, photograph by Richard Walker; pp. 8 (map), 11 Collection of the South Carolina Historical Society; pp. 8 (inset), 15, 16, 19, 20 courtesy of South Carolina Library, University of South Carolina, Columbia; p. 12 © Keren Su/CORBIS.

Krebs, Laurie.
A day in the life of a colonial indigo planter / by Laurie Krebs.—1st ed.
    p. cm. — (The library of living and working in colonial times)
  ISBN 0-8239-6229-6 (lib. bdg.)
1. Pinckney, Eliza Lucas, 1723–1793—Juvenile literature. 2. Women plantation owners—South Carolina—Biography—Juvenile literature. 3. Plantation owners—South Carolina—Biography—Juvenile literature. 4. Plantation life—South Carolina—History—18th century—Juvenile literature. 5. South Carolina—History—Colonial period, ca. 1600–1775—Juvenile literature. 6. Indigo industry—South Carolina—History—18th century—Juvenile literature. [1. Pinckney, Eliza Lucas, 1723–1793. 2. Plantation life. 3. Indigo industry—History. 4. South Carolina—History—Colonial period, ca. 1600–1775. 5. Women plantation owners.] I. Title. II. Series.
    F272.P64 K74 2003
    975.7'02'092—dc21   2001007251
Manufactured in the United States of America

Eliza Lucas Pinckney grew indigo on all three plantations that she owned during the eighteenth century. Descriptions of Eliza Pinckney's day-to-day responsibilities were fictionalized, but the details of making indigo dye are true.

Contents

Eliza Lucas Pinckney, Indigo Planter

At five o'clock on a warm July morning in 1745, Eliza Lucas Pinckney was up and dressed for the day. She had important work to do at the far end of her **plantation**, where the summer's first crop of indigo grew. Today she would oversee an important step in processing the indigo to create a rich, blue dye. The dye would be sent to **textile** mills in England. In colonial times, it was unusual for a woman, especially a wealthy one, to be responsible for such a difficult job. Even more unusual, Eliza was only 23 years old.

◄ *This view of Charleston, South Carolina, includes the house built in 1745–1746, by Charles Pinckney, Eliza's husband.*

A Young Girl with a Vision

Elizabeth Lucas was born in 1722, in Antigua, **West Indies**, and was educated in England. She was 16 when her family moved to Wappoo Plantation near Charleston, South Carolina. A year later, her father was called to serve in the British Army. Eliza was left in charge of her younger sister, her sickly mother, and her father's three plantations. Eliza had a good business sense, and a love for **agriculture**. She experimented with crops that could be sold in Europe and that could bring much needed money to the colonies.

This doll is wearing a dress made of silk spun by silkworms grown on Eliza Pinckney's farm. The painting (above) shows a typical colonial farm.

A Map of the PARISH of St STEPHEN, in CRAVEN COUNTY; Exhibiting a View of the several Places Proposable for making a NAVIGABLE CANAL, between SANTEE and COOPER RIVERS, from an Actual Survey By HENRY MOUZON Junr

A SCALE OF MILES AND CHAINS, 69½ Miles to a Degree

PART OF THE PARISH OF St JOHN

PART OF THE PARISH OF St JAMES

BERKLY COUNTY

CRAVEN COUN

WALL EYE SWAMP

HELL HOLE SWAMP

Sowing Seeds for the Future

Seated in her carriage, Eliza thought back to the start of her indigo project. Her father had sent indigo seeds from Antigua, hoping they would grow well in South Carolina's soil. Frost killed the first crop. Insects ruined the second harvest. A dye maker from the West Indies, sent to help, did not like working for a woman. He purposely ruined the third crop by adding too much **limewater** to the mix. Eliza **persisted**. By 1744, she produced indigo of fine quality. She also shared her seeds with neighbors who became indigo planters, too.

◀ *An old map of South Carolina shows an indigo farm. The drawing* (inset) *and photo show examples of indigo plants.*

Mrs. Charles Pinckney

As her carriage neared the indigo tubs, Eliza waved to her husband. In 1744, Colonel Charles Pinckney, a lawyer, had asked Eliza to marry him. Although she was only 23, and he was twice her age, their marriage proved to be a happy union. Together the Pinckneys owned at least four plantations and a grand home in Charleston, South Carolina. At Belmont Plantation, where Charles and Eliza lived, she continued her agricultural experiments. Eliza shared her love of plants with Charles.

This doll of Eliza Pinkney was created in 1995, by the South Carolina Historical Society. Eliza and Charles often traveled down the Ashley River, near their home, to attend parties. ▶

A Good Match

British trade was an important source of money for South Carolina. Indigo was an important ingredient for English textile mills. Eliza produced the indigo that was in great demand. Indigo planters **prospered** in South Carolina for other reasons, too. Rice, another important **export**, grew in low swamplands. Indigo grew well on higher ground. The two crops were harvested in different seasons. Farmwork was spread throughout the year. The slaves who harvested these crops were part of an endless supply of workers.

◀ *The silk cloth shown here has been dyed using indigo dye.*

Slavery in South Carolina

In colonial America, slavery was common, especially on southern plantations. Most slaves were people who had been taken from their homes in Africa. They were then brought to America and forced to do hard work on the plantations without any payment. Today we know that slavery is wrong. Now we have laws to protect a person's freedom, but, in Eliza's time, people were allowed to own slaves. Eliza had 25 men who harvested the indigo crop on her plantation. Their job was not pleasant. It was nasty, smelly work.

These drawings show slaves planting indigo plants (top) and tending to the young indigo plants (bottom). ▶

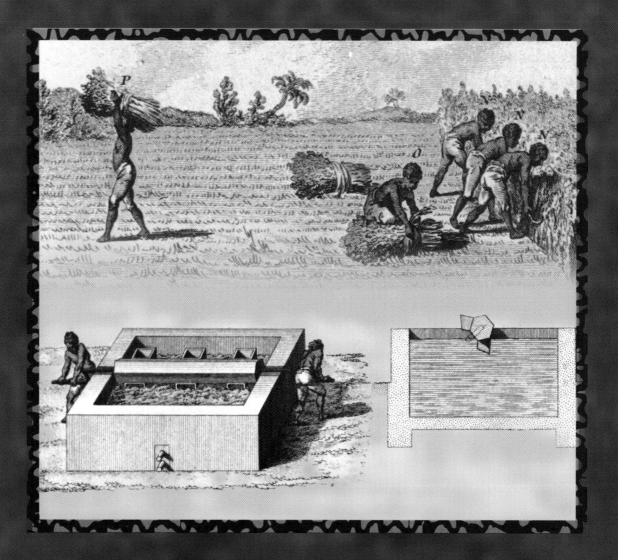

From Seed to Harvest

In March, the slaves planted indigo seeds in rows that were set 2 feet (.6 m) apart. In mid-July, the 3-foot (1-m) high plants were in full bloom. Their stalks had been cut and tied into large bunches. They were put to soak in steepers, which were tubs of water mixed with natural ingredients, including urine! Heavy logs kept the stalks under water. As Eliza looked into the upper row of tubs, she saw foaming yellow liquid. The plants were **fermenting** in the Carolina heat. The first step in making indigo was right on **schedule**.

◄ *These drawings show indigo being harvested* (top), *and then being soaked in tubs of water and natural ingredients.*

Into the Battery

A row of steepers sat above a row of tubs, called batteries. Fermenting liquid flowed from one level of tubs to the other. Eliza had a worker open drains on the top tubs. The foaming liquid ran down into the lower tubs. Slaves climbed into the batteries to beat the liquid with long, wooden paddles. The liquid turned from yellow to green. Eliza examined it closely. When blue specks appeared, the slaves added limewater. The blue **particles** then sank to the bottom of the batteries. Only solid indigo mud remained.

These are images of steepers and drains (top and middle), *dried indigo, and slaves beating indigo liquid* (bottom). ▶

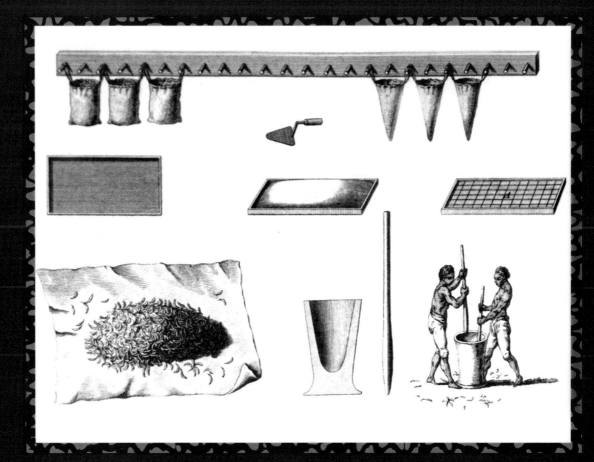

The Finished Product

The deep blue mud was scooped into linen bags and hung in the shade to dry into a thick paste. The dried indigo mud was spread on wide boards and placed on racks in a log house to dry completely. Weeks later, Eliza's indigo was cut into small, square cakes. Then the indigo was packed in barrels and shipped to Europe. By 1770, South Carolina shipped about 1 million pounds (453,592 kg) of indigo to Europe. Indigo was so prized by the British that planters, like Eliza, were paid a **bounty** if they sent the indigo just to England.

◀ *Indigo mud was dried for many weeks on racks that were placed in houses made of logs.*

Eliza's Place in History

Eliza Lucas Pinckney established South Carolina's indigo **industry**, but she had many other interests, too. She raised silkworms. A dress woven from Eliza's silk was made for Britain's Princess of Wales. Eliza was a talented musician, and she had studied law. She also held classes for the children of her slaves, so they could learn to read. On this warm July afternoon in 1745, as Eliza stepped back into her carriage, she had no idea that one day she would hold an important place in South Carolina's history.

Glossary

agriculture (A-grih-kul-cher) The science of producing crops and raising livestock, or animals.

bounty (BOWN-tee) Payment to encourage an industry.

export (ek-SPORT) To send something to another place to be sold.

fermenting (fur-MENT-ing) A chemical change that makes gas bubbles.

industry (IN-dus-tree) A moneymaking business in which many people work and make money producing a particular product.

limewater (LYM-wah-ter) Water with a high level of calcium in it.

particles (PAR-tih-kuls) Small pieces of something.

persisted (per-SIST-ed) To have stood firm in spite of opposition.

plantation (plan-TAY-shun) A very large farm where crops were grown.

prospered (PRAHS-purd) To have been successful.

quality (KWAH-luh-tee) A degree of excellence. A trait or characteristic of a person or thing.

schedule (SKEH-jool) A fixed time, an agenda.

textile (TEK-styl) Woven fabric or cloth.

West Indies (WEST IN-deez) The islands lying between southeastern North America and northern South America, bordering the Caribbean.

Index

Primary Sources

Cover (background). *Photo by Kirsten Soderlind (1977).* **(inset and page 11)** Detail from *"Down the dark Ashley River in a canoe from a great cypress."* A painting by Charles Copeland. From *The Dames and Daughters of Colonial Days*, by Geraldine Brooks (1900). **Page 4.** *Painting and a detail from* View of Charles Town, *Oil painting by Thomas Leitch (1774).* Early Southern Decorative Arts, Winston Salem, North Carolina. **Page 7.** *Doll showing gold damask, silk dress spun on Eliza Pinckney's plantation.* From the Smithsonian. **(inset).** *Colonial farm titled,* Van Bergen Overmantel, *oil painting by John Heaten (1773).* Fenimore Art Museum, Cooperstown, NY. **Page 8.** *Map of South Carolina's counties.* South Carolina Historical Society. **(background).** *Wild indigo plants photographed by Kirsten Soderlind (1997).* **(inset).** *Drawings of indigo plants.* From The South Carolina Library. **Page 11.** *Eliza Pinckney doll.* Created in 1995, for the South Carolina Historical Society as part of the Great Women of South Carolina doll series. **Pages 15, 16, 19, 20.** *Drawings from the book,* L'art de l'indiotier *(1770).* From University of South Carolina. **Page 15.** *Drawing of slaves planting and tending to indigo plants..* **Page 16.** *Drawings of slaves harvesting indigo plants, and soaking them in tubs..* **Page 19.** *Drawings of steepers, drainers, dried indigo buds, and slaves crushing the indigo.* **Page 20:** *Drawing of log sheds where indigo is dried.*

Web Sites

Due to the changing nature of Internet links, PowerKids Press has developed an online list of Web sites related to the subject of this book. This site is updated regularly. Please use this link to access the list:
www.powerkidslinks.com/llwct/dlicinpl/